No Wheelchairs in Heaven

Myles De Vos' Courageous 21-Year Struggle
With Duchenne Muscular Dystrophy

No Wheelchairs in Heaven. Copyright © 2010 by Myrtle De Vos. All rights reserved. No part of this book may be used or reproduced in any manner whatsoever without written permission from the author, except in the case of brief quotations embodied in critical articles or reviews.

"Reflections on Rocky 02" (page 42) was first printed in the newsletter of American Reformed Church of Orange City. It is reprinted by permission of Mandy Lundberg.

"DeVos to make a dream trip" (page 18-19) first appeared in *The Daily Globe*, Worthington, MN. Reprinted with permission.

"In memory" (page 50) first appeared in *The Capital Democrat*. Reprinted by permission of Jeff Bylsma.

"Flippin' the flapjacks" (page 13) first appeared in *The Capital Democrat*. Reprinted by permission of Brian Wassenaar.

"Persecution Night" (pages 31-32) and "Sitting in the Rain" (page 26) first appeared in *The Capital Democrat*. Reprinted by permission of Janine Calsbeek.

Scripture quotations marked "The Living Bible" are taken from The Living Bible, Kenneth N. Taylor, Tyndale House, ©1971 by Tyndale House Publishers, Inc. Used by permission. All rights reserved.

Scripture quotations marked "New Inspirational Study Bible" are taken from the New King James Version. Copyright © 1982 by Thomas Nelson, Inc. Used by permission. All rights reserved.

ISBN: 978-0-9825974-5-3

Published and printed in the United States of America by The Write Place. Cover and interior design by Kathie Evenhouse, The Write Place. For more information, please contact:

The Write Place | 709 Main St., Suite 2 | Pella, Iowa 50219
www.thewriteplace.biz

Copies of this book may be ordered from The Write Place online at www.thewriteplace.biz/bookplace

This book is dedicated to anyone who has or has had Duchenne Muscular Dystrophy.

Table of Contents

No Wheelchairs in Heaven 2

Acknowledgments 3

Introduction 5

1   The Early Years 7

2   Give Myles a Lift 11

3   Make a Wish 15

4   Through the Years 19

5   More About Myles 23

6   Persecution Night 29

7   The Night Myles Died 31

8   The Funeral 35

9   Sympathy Cards 43

10   The Memories Go On 47

11   Thoughts from Friend Jon DeKoster 51

12   Grant Lubbers' Essay 55

13   Thoughts from Myles' Mother, Kathy Heronemus 59

14   Sean's Poem 61

15   Through Myles' Eyes 65

No Wheelchairs in Heaven

Life isn't always easy
Sitting in a wheelchair
Sometimes I get discouraged
And loaded down with care

That's when I lean on Jesus
To help me through the day
For He gives me peace and comfort
When trials come my way

The Bible says there is a place
That someday I will see
Where there will be no sickness
Or pain to bother me.

I'll walk upon a street of gold
Glorious beauty I will share
In a place called Heaven
Where I'll need no wheelchair

J. Morse 1997

Acknowledgments:

This book would not have been possible without the help of Peg Juffer. I attended her writing class at the Landsmeer Ridge Retirement Center. She asked me why I was there and I said I wanted to write a book about my grandson, Myles. Shortly after that, she offered to help me. She spent many, many hours compiling this information with me. Thank you, Peg!

I also want to thank my husband, Herm, for his patience with me during this time.

Thanks also to Myles' mother, Kathy Heronemus; step-brother Sean Heronemus; and father Jeff De Vos and his wife, Tammy.

Thank you to Myles' special friends: Jon "Deke," John, Josh, Grant, Megan, and Kayla and all the others who were there for him. Without all of these, there would be no book.

And my thanks to J. Morse for the poem "No Wheelchairs in Heaven." I've never met you, and I tried hard to find you—without success. Thanks much for your poem. It touched me, and I'm sure it will touch the lives of other readers also.

Introduction:

Muscular dystrophy is a progressive hereditary disease, characterized by increasing muscle weakness. Caused by the absence of a key protein needed for muscle function, it occurs in several different forms.

My grandson Myles' form of muscular dystrophy was the most common one: Duchenne dystrophy, which usually results in symptoms before age five. Although it is caused by a defective gene for Dystrophin (a protein in muscles), it can occur in people without a known family history of the disease. It is passed by a gene on the x chromosome from a child's mother. Males most commonly develop symptoms, but females can be carriers without developing symptoms. It occurs in one of every 3,600 male infants.

Early symptoms include awkward walking, stepping or running, and frequent falls, as well as fatigue. Symptoms also include difficulty raising arms above the head and a curvature of the lower spine. A wheelchair is usually needed by adolescence.

It typically causes death by age 25, often from a lung disorder such as pneumonia—because breathing muscles are weakened.

Although research is being done, there is no known cure. The Muscular Dystrophy Association is an excellent source of information and support for people with muscular dystrophy and their families.

No Wheelchairs in Heaven

Myles De Vos' Courageous 21-Year Struggle With Duchenne Muscular Dystrophy

By Myrtle De Vos

The Early Years

My main purpose in writing this book is to share with children, teenagers, young adults, and anyone who could be a help to someone who is handicapped.

My grandson, Myles, was diagnosed with Duchenne Muscular Dystrophy when he was about four years old. He was born a healthy-looking, cute-as-can-be baby. When he was nearly four, he was seen by an Iowa City doctor because he was very short. Doctors considered giving him growth hormones. After a few visits, they noticed his walk was unusual. They took a sample of muscle from his hip and discovered the MD. Duchenne MD is a genetic condition and is passed on through the mother.

Shortly after Myles was diagnosed, our minister had a

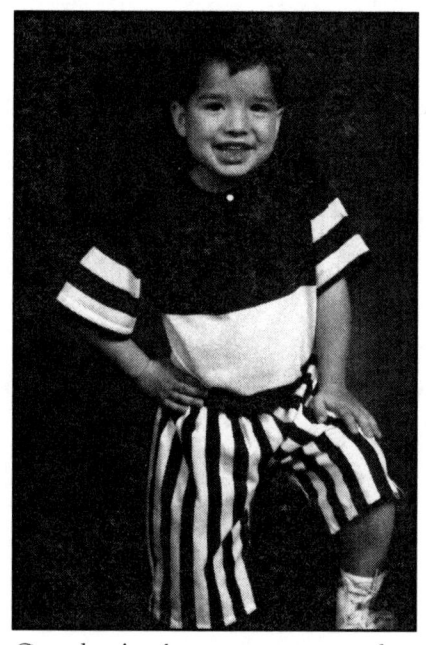

Grandma's favorite picture taken when Myles was four years old.

sermon based on the Bible Scripture, "Those who wait on the Lord shall renew their strength. They shall mount up with wings as eagles. They shall run and not be weary; they shall walk and not faint" (Isaiah 40:31, *The Inspirational Study Bible*). The sermon was about a young boy who was very ill. One day, his Sunday school teacher came to visit. When he left, the boy called to his mother. When she came, he lifted a Kleenex box and said, "Look, Mom, I'm strong." Then he died. It made me very sad but the Scripture became my Scripture for Myles the rest of his life. Another Scripture that has been a big part of my life is from II Corinthians 1:3-4 (*The Living Bible*). "What a wonderful God we have, who so wonderfully strengthens us in our hardships and trials. And why does He do this, so that when others are troubled, needing our sympathy and encouragement, we can pass on to them this same help and comfort God has given us." I carry this passage in my wallet daily.

Myles' mother, Kathy, again became pregnant. So it was suggested she have an amniocentesis. She learned it was going to be a girl. Only boys can develop Duchenne MD. Either way they would not have terminated the pregnancy. The new baby girl was named Nicole. She was called Nikki.

The Iowa City doctor wanted Myles to start taking prednisone, which would have slowed down the muscle weakness but would not stop it from progressing. Myles' parents decided not to give it to him because there were too many side effects and would most likely cause him to gain weight and get puffy.

Myles started school going mornings to a special school in Rock Valley and afternoons to kindergarten in Sioux Center. The rest of his school years were at MOC-Floyd Valley.

His parents divorced and Myles went to live with his father Jeff and Nikki lived with her mother Kathy. Myles spent many weekends and summer days with his mom.

A couple of Labor Day weekends, I took calls from community members for the Jerry Lewis Telethon. I was very impressed when several children called to say they were in Myles' class in school and wanted to pledge five dollars. From the very beginning, the children cared about Myles. Grant Lubbers, another student, carried him up the stairs to a special education class. The teachers told the kids to play games Myles could play. Later, he even played touch football from his wheelchair. Jeff went before the school board to request an elevator, which was installed.

For some time, Jeff brought Myles to my house to sleep and I brought him to school in the morning. It became a game — every night just after Jeff left, Myles called out, "Grandma." I went into the bedroom and said, "What do you want Myles?" His answer was always, "It starts with a D and ends with a K." He wanted a drink. Night after night, the same. It became our little joke because he finally couldn't say it without breaking down laughing.

Give Myles a Lift

When Myles was in fourth grade, eleven years old, he became confined to a wheelchair. Some of Jeff's co-workers decided to do a benefit to earn money to buy a lift for the van.

Flippin' the Flapjacks
by Bryan Wassenaar

Last Friday evening's benefit pancake supper for Myles De Vos, a rural Orange City youth stricken with muscular dystrophy, drew 680 area residents and others to the supper tables of Orange City's Adult Activity Center, where the same consumed over 2,720 pancakes, 70 lbs. of sausages, 13 gallons of pancake syrup, and 39 lbs. of margarine.

A craft sale, pie auction, silent auction, and raffle aided in the success of the event by bringing in over $7,500.00, a sum which will be used to purchase a wheelchair lift for Myles.

In the meantime, Aunt Val heard about a boy who had some treatments at The Ward Chiropractic Clinic in Long Beach, California. So Jeff, Grandpa Herm, and Myles made the trip. Myles came back sitting straighter and with a much better attitude. Jeff asked the doctor if he would consider coming to Orange City to show Dr. Stange some of his techniques. He agreed to do this if they would pay his airfare and motel and also give him a home-cooked meal. Some of Myles' benefit money was used for this. Myles saw Dr. Stange quite often after that.

While Myles and his dad and grandpa were in California, they stopped at the Crystal Cathedral. Myles' comment before going was, "I don't want to go to no church." He changed his mind when he got there.

The security guard showed them around but there was a wedding so he couldn't take them up in the tower that day. He said, "Why don't you come back on Sunday?" That was the day of the Easter production, "Glory of Easter."

Herm said, "We tried to get tickets, but there weren't any."

So the guard, Ted, said, "Wait right here." He came back with tickets in the fifth row. They went to see the production on Sunday. Myles couldn't go to the animals so they brought them to him right during the production.

Shortly after they were back in Iowa, Jeff's co-workers held the benefit, a pancake feed and auction on many donated items. Some 7th and 8th grade students from the Alton Middle School My Choice Program also had a carnival to earn money for Myles to equip the van with accessories to accommodate the wheelchair. They presented him with a check in the amount of $225.

Jim Hunt, a community member, had his hair cut. The braids

were sold at $10 a piece. This money was also donated to the lift fund.

Myles also received a donation from Buddy Adler, one of the actors in the Crystal Cathedral's Easter production, along with a picture of Myles and him.

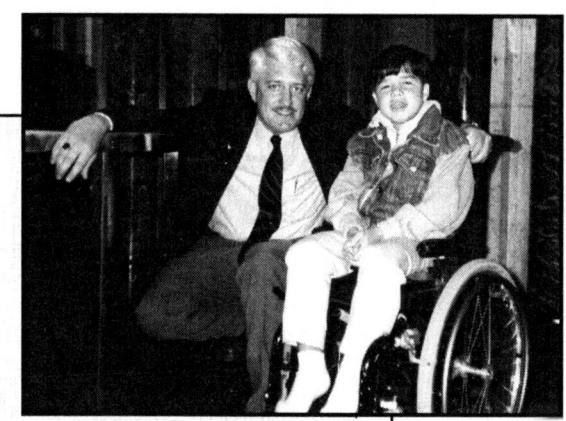

Arthur C. Buddy Adler
P.O. Box 1864
Studio City Station
North Hollywood, California 91614-0664
SAG. AFTRA. AEA.

May 14, 1993

Dear Myles,

You made my whole day when I met you during The Glory Of Easter Production at the Crystal Cathedral Church outside under the East Balcony.

You are a very courageous young man and I cant tell you how much I admire your great spirit and your Faith. I could see in the smile on your face and the sparkle in your eyes, that you already know that Jesus will always be your Friend.

I have enclosed a check for you to use as you see fit.

I am a Professional Character Actor from Hollywood, Ca. and am the longest surviving Actor in the Combined Glory Productions. This year was my tenth anniversary in the Glory Productions, ten years in The Glory Of Christmas and ten years in the Glory Of Easter in seven different lead Roles in 1270 consecutive Performances without ever missing a single one before over 2.75 Million People in the twenty Productions and ten Seasons.

I will keep you in my Prayers and God Bless you always.
Sincerely yours,
Buddy Adler
403 Ohio Ave. N.W.
Orange City, Iowa 51041

Make a Wish

There was at least one of Myles' wishes that was granted.

When Myles was eleven, his mother, Kathy, contacted John Stivers in Sioux City to ask about the Make-A-Wish Foundation. She had seen the name in a newspaper. She was surprised that Myles was selected out of all the requests it received.

After Kathy was called back, there was an interview with Myles and it had to be confirmed through a physician that he was suffering from muscular dystrophy.

In February, Myles, Kathy, and her family went to the Daytona 500. Myles' dad Jeff races figure eights and some oval track. His stepfather, Michael Heronemus, does mini-sprints. So, it was Myles' wish to see Daytona 500 and meet race car driver Kyle Petty.

Myles talked with his favorite driver and several others. "He was escorted into the pit area with flashing lights and everything," said Kathy. "A lot of people would give anything to get in the pits and meet some of the drivers."

Myles was all smiles that day. He said, "I'm going to be famous. Everybody is paying attention to me."

Make-A-Wish Foundation helps...

De Vos to make a dream trip

by Rosalie Block

Myles De Vos, 11½-year-old son of Michael and Kathy Heronemus, Ashton, and Jeff and Tammy De Vos, Orange City, will have one wish answered this week.

He and his mother, Kathy Heronemus, his step-father, Michael Heronemus, and Myles' 5-year-old sister, Nikki De Vos, will leave Friday for Daytona, Fla. and watch the Daytona 500. Not only will they see the NASCAR race, they will meet Kyle Petty, the son of Richard Petty, who recently retired from racing.

All of this is possible through the Make a Wish Foundation, an organization dedicated to making the wishes come true of children affected by life-threatening disease.

While the family is thrilled to be attending the prestigious racing event, it is only one wish that will be fulfilled. Another, even larger dream, is that soon a cure will be found for muscular dystrophy, the degenerative muscle disease that has caused Myles to depend upon a wheelchair while he attends school at Maurice-Orange City.

Myles still asks why he is unable to run, to ride a bicycle, to do the active outdoors things that other children his age can do, says his mother.

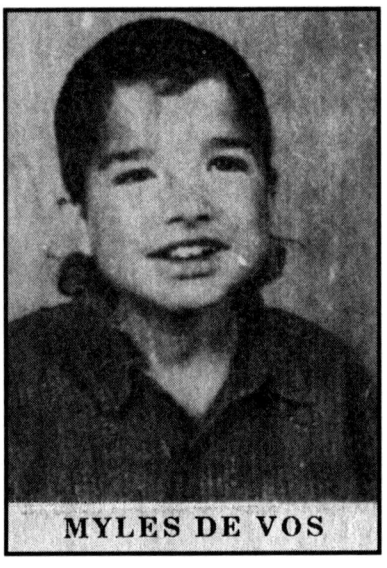

MYLES DE VOS

A boy's wish will come true

That makes it hard for everyone, she admitted, and it is especially difficult for her not to see her son every day, since he stays with his father during the week.

"But I tell him that we have to keep praying and hoping that there is a chance," said Kathy, adding that it seems that research is close to finding answers.

"We just don't know if it will be in time," she said.

continued on next page

The family learned that Myles had muscular dystrophy when he was about 3 years old. He had difficulty walking, and he could never ride a bicycle.

A specialist in Spencer sent Myles and his family to Iowa City, where it was confirmed through a muscle biopsy that he had muscular dystrophy.

There are many types; Myles has Duchenne, which is the worst, said Kathy. It affects boys, so there is little chance that Nikki would ever be afflicted. It was learned that Kathy carries the defective gene, so with the birth of her second son, Sean Heronemus, 6-months-old, there is a concern.

"We just haven't wanted to find out, yet," she admitted. "We just can't face it yet."

Kathy can see that Myles does seem to become a little weaker as time goes on. He still is able to walk, but it is the first year that he has had to rely on a wheelchair in school. It is important that exercising of his muscles is done every day.

Even though she does not see him every day, Kathy is working hard to do what she can for her son. She has placed his name on lists for hospitals that do research for the disease, and she keeps in touch with doctors and families of other sufferers.

She would like to answer other wishes that Myles has — such as meeting Michael Jordan some day, or possibly Garth Brooks.

"I intend to do everything possible for him, even if he's not always with me," she said.

She and her family are grateful for all those who help support the Muscular Dystrophy Association (MDA) during fund drives. Through MDA, Myles has received financial help in getting equipment that he needs.

Kathy contacted John Stivers in Sioux City to ask about the Make A Wish Foundation. She had seen the name in an area newspaper. She was surprised that Myles was selected out of all the requests they receive. Anyone else who might want to find out if they would qualify could call Stivers, she said. The number is (712) 276-3004.

After Kathy was called back, there was an interview with Myles and it had to be confirmed through a physical that he was suffering from muscular dystrophy.

While the trip is going to be exciting, there is still much that remains to be done to see that Myles leads as fulfilling a life as possible.

In the meantime, said his mother, "He struggles each day to be normal."

Through the Years

Finally, Myles was in MOC-Floyd Valley High School. His first homecoming date as a freshman was Megan Stange. She had to come to our house to pick him up. Grandpa Herm had to show her how to use the wheelchair lift on Myles' family van. After the dance, she also brought him back to our house. I thanked her for all she did. The next day, she told her

First homecoming date

father, "Myles' grandmother kept thanking me, but I wanted to do it. He's my friend."

Myles' junior prom date was Kayla Maassen. Some girls asked her why she wanted to go with him because she couldn't dance the way she would like to. This shows that some people do good things in spite of peer pressure.

Myles attended the youth group, First Impact, at First Reformed Church throughout his teen years. He then decided he wanted to

Junior prom date

go to TEC, which is Teens Encounter Christ, and held at different churches in the area. He sent in his registration and money, however the organization returned it and explained that it couldn't accommodate a handicapped person, but members of his youth group said, "Myles is going. Jon (Deke) can go as a worker and they can communicate by walkie-talkie. Jon can help him take care of all his personal needs."

At this TEC, Myles met Kayla Faber. After that she came to Orange City several times and took him out to eat or to a movie. Later on, Megan Stange also took him to some movies.

At one family Christmas present exchange, the phone rang and it was Megan. She wanted to know when Myles would be available because she wanted to take him to a movie. Of course Myles was excited to go. Anything with Megan was great.

When Myles was a senior, he found out he was going to have to wear a back brace. His stepmother, Tammy, had been to school to discuss this with personnel. Afterwards, she was at our house telling him he would need more help because he wouldn't be able to reach as far. A big tear fell down each of his cheeks. He sadly said, "I feel so useless."

As I watched, I thought, "Oh, boy, what now?"

After just a bit I said, "Myles, look at it this way, when someone is helping you, you are helping them to feel good about themselves." He wiped the tears away. Sometime later he went on a mission trip to Benton Harbor, Michigan, with First Impact. After he came back, he was having supper at our house and he said, "Grandma, on this trip I let people help me and I didn't feel bad about it."

Myles attended TEC several times. The last time was in Spencer, Iowa. On Saturday night, he started to choke at suppertime. Jon (Deke) had to take him to the local emergency room. Can you picture all these kids praying for him while he's gone? When he came back and they saw he was okay, they asked him what he had to say. He said, "I don't have a date yet for senior prom. Does anyone want to volunteer?" A girl from Hartley, Cassy (Mohni) Bohnet, went to the prom with him.

Again, Grandpa Herm had to wash the van and the wheelchair. Myles sat in a lawn chair telling him where he missed a spot or two. Then John Hofmeyer drove on the driveway and asked if Myles wanted to go cruising for a while. I asked John to be back in one-half hour and if he wanted to stay for supper, which he did. We were just finished with supper when the doorbell rang. It was Jon (Deke) and another friend to pick him up to go to town to pick up their tuxes. What guy in Myles' condition would have these privileges? Travis Plathe, a special friend, was always Myles' chauffeur.

Myles invited Megan to be his date at the senior winter ball. Again, she had to pick him up and drive the van. Myles was selected Winter Ball king. Katie Van Voorst was Winter Ball queen.

More About Myles

Ditch Story

One evening after a football game, Myles was supposed to go home with his brother, K.C., but Myles said he could get home by himself riding in his wheelchair from the stadium. However, it got late and he still wasn't home.

Jeff needed to get to bed because he had to get up early so he went to look for Myles. As he left the driveway, a pickup slowed down and stopped to look in the ditch and then drove on. This prompted Jeff to look in the ditch also.

It was so dark he had to feel his way. He came upon the wheelchair and it was empty. He hollered, "Myles, let me know if you are there." After about four calls, Jeff heard a faint cry for help. It was coming from under the wheelchair. Myles said he saw the pickup coming and turned into the ditch.

Jeff took him home and he wasn't hurt.

My Tour of Homes

We moved to a new home that was renovated from an old hatchery. Many people wanted to see our home, so I decided to hold my own tour where we collected donations for the Jerry Lewis

Telethon. Myles was the greeter at the door. Even the company who installed our house siding made a donation. Then, Myles, Nikki, and I went to the TV station in Sioux City, Iowa, while the telethon was being held and donated the $1,000 we had collected. We thought that was a pretty good day's work.

Sitting in the Rain

According to Jeff and his wife, Tammy, huge numbers of people in town would do anything for Myles.

How about the time when Myles' wheelchair battery ran out of juice? It was drizzling. So, Mrs. Leonard Krommendyk called the De Vos home, then headed outside with an umbrella and some milk and cookies. She held the umbrella over Myles while he waited.

At school, all sorts of kids helped—like Jon DeKoster, John Hofmeyer and Grant Lubbers—doing everyday things. And after school, DeKoster, also a senior at MOC-Floyd Valley High, drove Myles to his favorite sports, like the races.

Lubbers drove Myles to the Iowa vs. Drake basketball game on Tuesday, Nov. 21, 1999, in Des Moines, Iowa. Loren DeJong's high school business management class earned money at the volleyball pack-the-gym night. And the class decided that year to use the money to send Myles to an Iowa game.

Myles and three of his friends—Lubbers, Nate Owens, and Andy Herda—went to the game that Tuesday.

Are all these kids good friends? Or just good kids?

Both, said Myles and his family.

Sitting in the Rain, by Janine Calsbeek
published in the Orange City, Iowa,
newspaper, *Capital Democrat*

Getting His Way

Myles' dad, Jeff, said Myles would never come right out and ask for anything. For instance, if he wanted a drink, Myles would say, "I sure am thirsty." He would never just say, "Please, would you get me a drink?"

So... once Myles saw a TV set at Pamida. Jeff would have gladly given him the money to buy it, but he wanted Myles to ask for it. Finally, Jeff told him that maybe Grandpa Herm would lend him the money. So, Myles rode his wheelchair the mile and a half into town. Herm was washing the car, so Myles followed him around the car saying, "They have this nice TV set at Pamida. It sure would be nice to have because then I could change my own channels." Again, he didn't come right out and ask for it.

After some time, Herm couldn't stand it anymore, and he said, "Would you like to borrow the money from Grandpa?"

Myles said, "Could I?"

Then Jeff had to bring the van into town so Herm could take Myles in his wheelchair to purchase that TV.

Once again, Myles got his way without directly asking for something.

Open Campus

When Myles was a senior, his school had an open campus. Almost every Thursday evening he called and asked for Grandpa, "Gramps, are we going for noon lunch tomorrow?"

Myles always wanted to go to the Okey Dokey (the OK Café in Alton). It was hard to get the motorized wheelchair in there because of the steps, so Jeff made a small wooden wheelchair ramp. One of the owners, Tom, asked if Jeff would give him the pattern so he could make one like it. We told him it could stay there because it was the only place we used it. It is still there today even though the whole restaurant was recently remodeled.

Birthday Party

On Myles' eighteenth birthday, Herm and I took Myles and six or seven of his friends to the Pizza Hut. All was quiet until a group of teenage girls came and sat at a table next to us. Then they got just a little rowdy. We thought it was neat that this made it a typical teenage party.

Door Knocker

Myles often rode his wheelchair into town. Many Sundays he came to our house. Finally, he couldn't reach the doorbell so he banged his chair against the door so we would know he was there.

Favorites

Myles' favorite food was Keebler Wheat Crackers with Kraft Pimento Cheese Spread. His favorite movie was "Little Rascals," which he knew by heart and he imitated the characters. His favorite books were the "Curious George" books. He liked to watch NASCAR races and the weather channel. He could always tell you where there was bad weather or snow storms.

Ramp Incident

Once, Myles was seeing how close he could get to the edge of the ramp—up and down, up and down he would go. This finally resulted in a fall and a broken arm. He had a brace on that arm and he wanted to go to the figure-eight races at the track that night, so he said it didn't hurt.

Stuck at Home

It drove Myles wild when he was stuck at home and couldn't get the door open. So, he somehow used a bicycle inner tube to get the door open and left for town. His parents couldn't figure out how he got outside by himself.

Trip to Okoboji

One summer, a friend who had moved to New York, Nick Van Wyk, came to Orange City for a vacation. Nick's mom, Lori, and stepdad took Myles along to Arnolds Park at Lake Okoboji for a day. How thoughtful to spend part of your vacation making the day special for someone.

Persecution Night

Persecution Night

Sometimes "thank you" doesn't seem like enough. That's how Jeff and Tammy De Vos feel.

So many people have helped their son Myles through the years. How do you ever thank them enough?

The rest of the family agree—Holly, who's 9, and KC, 13, and also the Sheldon branch of the family—Kathy and Michael Heronemus, Nicole, 13, and Sean, 8.

Where else but Orange City would 300 people come out on a Thursday night and hunt for one kid?

It was "persecution night" with the First Reformed and Trinity youth groups—an event reminiscent of the persecution of the Jews, according to Jeff. The kids spread out and tried to sneak across town without being discovered by the "enemy."

Myles, dressed in black, hid too well; he didn't get discovered for two hours.

"The persecutors had to call out reinforcements," said Tammy with a smile.

When Myles didn't show up a half an hour after he was supposed to, people started to worry.

At 8:45 p.m., Tammy was sitting at the church waiting for Myles. Young people and parents started the search. By 9:30, the sheriff's department, the police department, the fire department, and the ambulance crew were on the scene. Neighbors and friends joined the search, too, even walking the ditches in case Myles had been hit by a car.

There were kids and parents searching with bikes, mopeds, cars, and trucks.

Around 10:30 p.m., Dan Hibma found Myles, who was stuck in a garden somewhere east of American Reformed Church.

Was he scared? Embarrassed?

"No," Myles said. "I was mad!"

"Now he wants a four-wheel drive wheelchair," said Jeff. Instead, Jeff and Tammy got him a cell phone.

This "persecution night" happened in late October of 1999.

"What are you going to pull next week?" Jeff asked Myles the following Monday. "It's been a while."

Persecution Night, by Janine Calsbeek
published in the Orange City, Iowa,
newspaper, *Capital Democrat*

The Night Myles Died

The night of July 27, 2002, will remain forever in my mind.

The evening started with Myles spending the weekend with his mother. Jeff took Nikki go-cart racing at Sheldon. When he dropped Nikki off at her mother's near Sheldon, Kathy came out and asked Jeff to come in and have a look at Myles because she was worried about him.

Jeff was alarmed at Myles' condition because his heart was racing really fast. Jeff said, "We need to get him to the hospital now." Jeff called us about midnight, waking us so we could get dressed. Then he and Tammy came over and waited at our house until Kathy and Myles arrived in Orange City.

They all proceeded to the Orange City Municipal Hospital. There, the doctors transferred him to Sioux Falls by ambulance. Before the ambulance left, Jeff called us so we could see Myles before he went to Sioux Falls. (The ambulance drivers were Mary and Willard VanVugt. Interestingly, Mary's mother also suffers with a type of MD.)

Myles' good friend, Jon DeKoster, was not only at the emergency room, he was right by the bed. Jeff asked him to stay behind and call some of Myles' friends. However, when everyone got to Sioux Falls about three in the morning, we found that Jon, John Hofmeyer, and Josh Dykstra had raced ahead of us. Then, Jon used his cell phone to call other friends.

Myles was put in the ICU for only a short time. The doctor told us that he was sleeping and that he might wake up and he might not. She gave him two to forty-eight hours to live. He was transferred to a private room where he was given oxygen. The doctor said the oxygen really wasn't doing him any good so it was removed.

Even though Myles was twenty-one, he was short of stature. Even so, it was surprising yet special to go into the room and see his mother, Kathy, holding him across her lap while she sobbed. After a while, she laid him on the bed.

We were in the room and saw Jon standing by the bed. He was actually able to get Myles to speak. The rest of us flocked to the bed to see if we could get him to speak.

Jeff was sitting on the bed and Myles said, "Ouch."

"What's wrong?" Jeff asked.

"You're sitting on my leg," Myles complained.

"Well, if I can get you to talk, I'll do it again," remarked Jeff.

By Sunday morning, several students and a couple of teachers had arrived and everyone crowded into the room. Megan Stange came all the way from Lake Okoboji. She hadn't bothered to change from her swimming suit but had just put a shirt over it. Megan and Jon were the only two friends who stayed with us to the end.

One of the special nurses wanted to hear all of Myles' stories. She even said, "It's okay to fill the hallway with friends and relatives." She lightened our burden somewhat.

Sometime during the day, I went to the gift shop and found two little cards that contained a Scripture that had always been special to me because it spoke to Myles' condition. I gave one to Jeff and one to Kathy.

On Sunday afternoon, Herm and I decided to go to a motel to get a little sleep. However, I was too restless and soon went back to the hospital. Herm followed a short time later.

I decided to lie down on a hospital couch for a while. Kathy was in the hospital lobby and Jeff had gone back to the motel to get some rest. In the meantime, Herm was in the room and told Megan that she should find something to eat. While they were both out of the room, Myles slipped peacefully away at midnight. That prompted Megan to say when she returned, "That stinker slipped out on me."

Sadly everyone returned home. Now the work of planning a funeral had to begin.

The Funeral

Herm and I were asked to be present while planning the funeral service. Mr. Oolman, the funeral director, asked if there was special Scripture we wanted on the program. Kathy's husband, Michael, said he would like the Scripture I gave them in the hospital, which was from Isaiah 40:31 (*The Inspirational Study Bible*):

"Those who wait upon the Lord shall renew their strength. They shall mount up with wings as eagles. They shall run and not be weary; they shall walk, and not faint."

Notes written on the casket

It was time to choose the coffin. Mr. Oolman gave us several choices. It was a unanimous decision. We chose one with an entire lid you could write on. I had never seen or heard of this type of coffin before. The night of the visitation, the entire lid was covered with sentiments from friends and family. I wrote, "It starts with a D and ends with a K," referring to that ritual many years before that was special to Myles and me. Megan wrote, "You showed me love, friendship, dedication, optimism, and integrity. You'll forever be my favorite dancing partner. I'll love you forever."

At the visitation, Megan and Kayla Faber were visiting with each other. I went up and asked them if they were ever jealous of each other. They just grinned and said that they were a part of Myles' life at different times.

John Block, the First Reformed Church youth director, was asked to perform the funeral service. He spoke of the time Myles went on a week-long mission to Benton Harbor, Michigan. This trip could only happen because good friend Jon (Deke) DeKoster went to help Myles with his needs. While there, they did the washing of

Good friends pay their last respects

feet. Myles was deeply touched. John Block mentioned in the message that this incident moved Myles so much that when he got home, it caused Tammy to say, "What did you do to my son?"

At the graveyard after the burial, friends and family gathered for some time. Weeping and hugging each other.

Myles Alan was the son of Jeffrey Dale and Kathy Jo (Jorgensen) De Vos. He was raised at Orange City, where he graduated from the M-OC Floyd Valley High School. He had completed his first year of computer technology at the Northwest Iowa Community College in Sheldon.

Myles was a member of the First Reformed Church and was active in TEC (Teens Encounter Christ). He enjoyed participating in the church's youth activities, especially their work project in Benton Harbor, Michigan.

He was an avid racing fan and admired NASCAR driver Dale Jarret. He liked to watch television, particularly weather forecasts and sports events.

As a victim of Duchenne muscular dystrophy, Myles was an inspiration to all who knew him. He touched countless lives, and the community responded to him in many ways. He appreciated the relationships he had with all his good friends.

Survivors include his parents, Jeffrey and Tammy De Vos of Orange City; and Kathy and Michael Heronemus of Sheldon; grandparents, Herman and Myrtle De Vos of Orange City; John and Beverly Phipps of Cherokee; Andrew and Wilmina Oostra of Rock Valley; and Elmer and Myrna Heronemus of Ashton; four brothers and sisters, K.C. De Vos, Nicole De Vos, Holly De Vos, and Sean Heronemus; and an honorary brother, Jon De Koster, of Orange City.

He was preceded in death by a grandfather, Leonard Jorgensen, Jr.

Memorials are being directed to the Myles De Vos account of the M-OC Floyd Valley Foundation, to make the school more accessible to the handicapped.

Following the committal service at the cemetery, relatives and friends are invited to join the family in the church fellowship hall for lunch and fellowship.

OOLMAN
FUNERAL HOMES

After the lunch at church, several friends decided to go to Sioux City and get tattoos with an M and wings. One of the girls' mothers wondered about when she fell in love, what her boyfriend would say. Her answer was, "If he doesn't understand, he doesn't love me."

Good friends pay their last respects

> "We are overwhelmed by your caring, your expressions of sympathy, food, and memorial gifts. We thank the Lord for allowing Myles to be such a special part of our lives. It is so hard to give Myles up, but we know he is in a better place with a new body!"
> ❧ Herm & Myrtle De Vos ☙

Thank you is simply not enough to say to express the feelings we have towards this community. We are thankful each and every day for the years we had with Myles, and we know that without your support, things would have been so much different. To the MOC-FV class of 2001, the T.E.C. community, and the countless dear friends we say a special "THANK YOU" for the many selfless acts of kindness that were shown to Myles and our family. It will never be forgotten. A special thank you to Rodney's Studios for their extra efforts in making and framing the large portrait of Myles at such short notice. Thank you as well for the contributions to the Myles DeVos Account of the MOC-FV Foundation. Your generosity will be used to help make the way easier for another student or students who may face hardship because of a disability.

Blessings in Disguise are Difficult to Recognize

God sends his "little angels"
In many forms and guises
They come as lovely miracles
That God alone devises.
For he does nothing without a purpose,
Everything's a perfect plan
To fulfill in bounteous measure
All he has ever promised man.
For every "little angel"
With a body bent and broken,
Or a little mind that's challenged
Or little words unspoken,
Is just God's way of trying
To reach and touch the hand
Of all who do not know Him
And cannot understand
That often through an angel
Whose wings will never fly
The Lord is pointing out the way
To his eternal sky.
Where there will be no handicaps
Of body, soul and mind
And where all limitations
Will be dropped and left behind
So accept these "little angels"
As gifts from God above
And thank him for this lesson
In faith and hope and love.

The family of Myles De Vos

Reflections On Rocky '02

ROCKY MOUNTAIN HIGH

We hit the road July 25 at 6:30 a.m. Armed with a duct-taped TV and lots of movies, we set out for Glenwood Springs, Colorado. While there, we visited Elizabeth Van Oort's relatives, went white water rafting, and toured a cave. Whether learning the area's history or just enjoying God's creation, we had fun and bonded as a group.

After a drive through Rocky Mountain National Park, we arrived at Rocky Mountain High Saturday evening. The theme verse this year is from Philippians 3:12-13, "I press on forgetting what is behind and straining towards what is ahead." What sticks out most in my mind about Rocky '02 is the fellowship with other Christians. As a graduate, it was fun to be able to enjoy time with other graduates before we go off to college. Not only did we have fun, but we got to grow in our relationship with Christ as well. I especially found it comforting to find people coing together in the midst of suffering. After hearing the news that Myles De Vos wasn't doing so well, a group of us came together to pray for him. It was really neat to see a group of kids give up some of their free time to commune together in prayer. There were a lot of people there, and it was an awesome sight to see.

Throughout Rocky, we listened to speakers and had group devotionals, which confirms my walk with God. During the evening sessions we had worship time with the Salty Dogs. It was a great experience to be surrounded by 2000 teenagers all worshiping the Lord. Yet, all things must come to an end, so we packed up and left for home on Wednesday morning.

As I prepare to leave for college, I just wanted to leave you with a few words of encouragement to say God is moving in the youth. Take care and God bless!

Love in Christ,
Mandy Lundberg

Sympathy Cards

From Grade School Teachers:

So many teachers were touched by Myles and were taught life lessons by him. He will be missed but we were blessed to have known him.

—Kim and Keatyn Bihrer

Myles will be remembered fondly. He was certainly a determined young man in my elementary music class.

—Sharon Foughty

From High School Coaches:

Myles was truly a blessing to all who met and knew him. He was always positive and an encouragement to me at all times. I thank God for the chance I had to know him.

—Lyle Lundgren and family

Want you to know that we've been thinking of you and praying for you. Myles was a pure joy to have around and will no doubt be missed by so many people.

—Coach De Jong and Family

From High School Teachers:

We just wanted to express our sympathy and offer our prayers to your family. We had the pleasure of working with Myles during his high school years. His smile was readily available and his spirit undefeatable. We are thankful to have known him.

—Doug and Marlene De Zeeuw

Please accept my sympathy and prayers. Myles was a very special person and I enjoyed him in school.

—Pat Hansen

You are in our thoughts and prayers at this time. Myles was an inspiration to his classmates and teachers. His courage and his spirit made us better people.

—Dale and Jean Boone

From Friends and Their Parents:

What a testimony Myles life was. He touched so many people through his disability, especially Jon's. What a blessing Myles was to our family. We loved to have him over. Jon has matured in so many ways because of Myles. Myles was a true friend to Jon.

We pray for peace for your family in the days ahead, knowing the Myles is safe in the arms of Jesus and he can do cartwheels now.

With all our love,

—Marv, Marlys, Mike, Jon, and Jenny

As the days pass you remain in my prayers. I trust that you are relying on our Heavenly Father for strength in Myles' absence and I hope that He is filling you with a sense of peace as we can't help but wonder why. I want to thank you all for allowing me to be a part of both Myles' life and his death. He taught me so much about loving life and loving others generously. Although he is no longer here, these lessons remain. I am a fuller person because of him. Thank you for raising him to be a strong Christian man. He was an inspiration to many, an example worth noting. In fact, I took the opportunity to mention Myles in my testimony to over 140 campers and counselors at a bonfire last Thursday night. I explained his love and the way Myles lived for Jesus, not knowing how much longer he would live. But all of our days are numbered, what good does it do to let one pass us by without appreciating it as a gift from our Lord. Why not try to love life for all its worth and love others until it hurts? There's no greater way to spend our time than furthering God's kingdom and what a blessing it is to celebrate life with our brothers and sisters in Christ.

I was very blessed by Myles' friendship and it was a blessing to know your family as well. I hope you'll keep in touch every now and then.

You have my prayers. If there's anything else you need, just ask. God's greatest blessing to all of you. With love in Him,

—Kayla Faber

(A special friend Myles met at Teens Encounter Christ)

Thinking of you today and remembering Myles—He was a very "Special" young man with a happy attitude, with a smile for all. He was an inspiration and a blessing to many! We are thankful to God that we were blessed by knowing Myles. We will miss him.

May the Lord of comfort surround you with His love and peace. We will keep you and your family in our prayers.

—Terry and Colette Hofmeyer

Myles will be remembered by us as someone who "lived his life to the fullest." He set such a great example for all of us and his friends by doing what "he could" and rarely complaining about what he "couldn't do." His Christian testimony will continue to touch all of us.

—Dave, Anita, Meg, Chris, and Curt Bomgaars

The Memories Go On

Our son, Brad's wife, Val, called the Rev. Van Oort Sunday morning before church started. His sermon that day was "Having a Good Day." Sometime into the sermon he said, "But Herm and Myrt De Vos are not having a good day," and went on to tell about Myles' death. Our feelings were mixed because he died so peacefully.

K.C., Myles' brother, and Jamie, his cousin, were both at Rocky Mountain High the day Myles was dying. Tammy's parents went to meet her sister. They all went to fetch K.C. and Jamie. Myles died before they got back. A number of years later, Brad, Jamie's father, had a heart attack and almost died. Two friends he was working with revived him and called 911. He spent two weeks in the Heart Hospital in Sioux Falls. Jamie spent a large amount of time there with him remembering not being home when Myles passed.

Myles had such good friends, and years after he died, they are still our friends. Every time I see Grant, I get a big hug even in the checkout lane at the grocery store or in front of residents at Landsmeer Ridge Retirement Community where he comes to see his grandma.

Herm and I are invited to their weddings where videos are often shown. At Deke's wedding, Myles was on at least eight of the slides.

When Deke thanked people for coming he said, "Two years ago today I lost my best friend and now I have a new best friend."

John Hofmeyer named his first child Cameron Myles. Megan showed several slides of Myles at her wedding.

Myles was honored at three different race tracks. When Deke raced go-carts, "Mooch, Myles De Vos, co-driver," was painted on the car opposite the driver's side.

In memory
Evan De Haan circles the track at Rapid Speedway on Friday evening, Aug. 2, flying the number 88, Dale Jarret's number, favorite driver of Myles De Vos. De Vos was also remembered at Park Jefferson in the same fashion on Saturday, August 3. (Photo by Jeff Bylsma)

Myles' memorial money was given to the MOC-Floyd Valley Middle School in Alton so it could install handicap doors.

Myles' wooden ramp is still at the entrance to the OK Café in Alton for any or all wheelchair-bound people to use.

I said hi to Deke the other day; "You always included Myles."

His answer, "When we didn't, he sure let us know."

At the basketball games, they carried him up to the top of the bleachers and he sent them down when he wanted something. What a mooch!

Myles will never be forgotten. We are so thankful for being able to share in his life.

Heaven's racetrack

Thoughts from Friend Jon DeKoster

Benton Harbor, Michigan

This was the longest Myles was away from home without a parent.

We met up with other high school students through Youth Works from Barrett, Minnesota. Myles rode in the front seat of the fifteen-passenger van, and four guys lifted his chair into the trailer.

We helped at Preschool Elementary Bible School and worked at a soup kitchen/homeless shelter. We also painted a house and did yard work.

Myles always wanted to be helping out like carrying all the supplies on the back of his wheelchair and on his lap.

We also had a fun day and went to the beach off Lake Michigan.

The last night before we left for home, we had a reflection of the week and we were told how we were "Jesus with skin on" this week by what we did to help others during the week. He washed the feet of those around him even though it was considered only a job for the lowest servant. We then washed each other's feet. While having his feet washed, Myles felt the calling to give his life to Jesus. We prayed for him and he accepted Jesus right there in front of us all. It was a beautiful thing to see.

Weeks later, I was asked by Tammy, "What did you do to Myles?" She went on to say, "I used to ask him a question and he would barely say anything. Now I can't get him to stop talking!"

Myles was on fire for Christ and he did not care who knew it. It was the end of "Shy Myles" as we knew him. He was a changed man.

T.E.C. at Sioux Center First Reformed Church

Months after Myles went to Benton Harbor, he attended his first of many TEC (Teens Encounter Christ) weekend retreats. He once again met many new friends and learned more about what it meant to be a Christian, also how his life's struggles could be made into a positive thing. His faith was growing by the day and he was meeting new friends who would be by his side forever.

Arena Cross

He went to Des Moines Vet's Auditorium to see Sean race his dirt bike. He stayed overnight at the AIB College of Business in the fraternity where Tyler, Monty and Nate lived.

Motocross- Minneapolis Metrodome

Myles loved racing and loved motocross. His younger brother, Sean, had been riding for years. Sean got the chance to ride in the KTM challenge before the Supercross race. I was invited along.

The next year we loaded up into the "Mooch Mobile" and headed for Minneapolis again. This time it was with a bunch of friends; John Hofmeyer, Josh Dykstra, Myles, and myself.

There was an autograph session that we went to with all of the riders.

We got autographs from all of the best riders; Jeremy McGrath, Ricky Carmichael, Ezra Lusk and Travis Pastrana. We, of course, went back the next year as well.

Grant Lubbers' Essay

Written for Christian Student/Athlete Award
January 2001

What has been the most impacting experience or event in your life, other that your personal relationship with Jesus Christ?

The most impacting experience in my life has been my friendship with my classmate, Myles De Vos. Myles has muscular dystrophy. He has given me inspiration and encouragement through his attitude towards life. He always has a smile on his face. I have a picture of him standing up in my locker that I look at every day and wish that I could give him the strength to walk again. He means the world to me. Because he loves sports, I play football for him. I know that if he were able to play, he would be out there giving his all for the team. I care about him so much. Myles is my inspiration in athletics and in life.

Another Essay from Grant

"For when I am weak, then I am strong." If you take this verse from II Corinthians 12:10 (*The Inspirational Study Bible*) out of its spiritual text and look at it in a physical one, it describes one of my best friends, Myles. Myles was born with muscular dystrophy, a disease that gradually weakens the body over time. In fifth grade, the doctors wanted him to start using a wheelchair. Myles was determined not to use the wheelchair. He even went to the extent of letting all the air out of the tires once so he wouldn't have to use it. And, the first few times we got him into the chair, he wouldn't let us push him. He had to push himself as far as he could before he would let us help him. By sixth and seventh grade, Myles was too weak to walk and was confined to his motorized wheelchair. Myles had a very determined personality; once he had his mind set on something, there was nothing that was going to change his mind, even if he knew it could be dangerous.

For example, it was a cool October night with the leaves turning to beautiful golds, reds, and yellows. There wasn't a star in the sky, not even the moon. It was perfect, perfect because it was Persecution Night for all the youth groups in the area. You know the scene, all the youth group members scattering throughout the town to reach a secret meeting place to worship as they try to evade the secret police (the adults) who try to keep them from successfully completing their mission. Kids are running through yards, down alleyways, and hiding behind anything they can find, just to escape getting caught. Now picture Myles gliding across the streets and sidewalks with his black motorized wheelchair. His task is a little more difficult than the others since he cannot do all the maneuvers his friends are able to do, but he is determined to complete the mission. Suddenly, adults appear and everyone scatters. Then Myles decides to go off-roading and cuts through a yard. All of a sudden, his wheelchair comes to a halt, but his wheels are still spinning. He had found his way into a freshly tilled garden. It took the police and fire department as well as half of Orange City two hours to find him that night. Myles knew the risks of driving through yards with his wheelchair, but he took that risk knowing that if anything happened, he wouldn't be able to help himself. That was Myles' personality, always doing things that he probably shouldn't do, but doing them anyway because he was going to do his best in everything he did.

Myles never felt bad for himself and kept a very positive attitude toward life. Nothing was going to stop him from doing anything. He was going to do as much as he could by himself before he would let anyone help him. Myles may not have been strong in his body, but he was strong mentally and emotionally. He was as determined and stubborn as an ox. He wouldn't let anyone treat him differently just because he was in a wheelchair. I know of one instance when he actually chewed out one of his friends because he thought he was treating him special because of the wheelchair. Myles just wanted to be one of the guys, and he was. We treated him just like anyone else in the group. We made fun of him just like we did everyone else, and he loved us for it.

Myles knew he was handicapped, but he didn't let that keep him from experiencing life. He went to every car race and sporting event that he could. He worked hard in school and never gave up. He was going to college for computer programming and was getting ready to go back for another year. Then, on July 27, 2002, Myles was taken to the local hospital, then transferred to Sioux Falls where he passed away early in the morning of July 29. He was fighting the whole way up to the end. Most people with muscular dystrophy end up in the hospital for months before they pass away. But not Myles; he wouldn't go out that way. He was going to live his life to the fullest and take advantage of every opportunity that came along right up to the very end. So, on a beautiful, sunny August morning, we laid to rest the strongest man I have ever known.

Thoughts from Myles' Mother, Kathy Heronemus

Let's see where to start. When Myles was born, he was the most beautiful baby a mother could want. He had so much black hair and a dark complexion. He was perfect. I found out differently four years later.

Finding out that Myles had the deadly disease, Duchenne muscular dystrophy, that would one day kill him, was very hard to accept. I just kept denying that anything was wrong. I prayed that the doctors would find a cure before the time for Myles to leave us would come. Every day I kept up on new developments with his disease. My prayers on every doctor appointment that a cure could be found were never answered.

One day, I woke up and decided we needed to start making memories with Myles, and I needed to quit feeling sorry for myself. That's just what I started doing.

Life got easier because of accepting that Myles had this disease. Knowing one day he would no longer be with us was always hard. There's never a right time, no matter how many memories you make.

Myles lived a very fulfilled life with his family and many friends making sure of it. As a parent, it's hard sometimes to let a child with a handicap experience adventure, but I think that is a big part of what makes them keep going and not give up. At least that's what kept Myles going—the chance to be as normal as possible from a wheelchair. He got to experience almost everything a normal child gets to—trust me, his friends saw to that. They treated him just like one of the boys. Myles always had the "be as normal as I can be" attitude.

Myles was my inspiration and still is, not only for me but for a lot of others, also. I miss him a lot and think about him every day. Thank God for all the memories I did get to have with him. Some parents don't get that chance. I consider myself lucky to have had a child like Myles to teach me many things about life.

Myles always had a smile on his face no matter what. None of us could really know what it must have been like in his shoes. He never complained or ever let his disease bring him down.

Sean's Poem

Written by Myles' brother, Sean Heronemus, in 2009 when Sean was 17 years old.

Sometimes I sit here and ask myself why
What's the reason I don't even try
Maybe because I'm so wound up inside
I'll probably never reach my dreams.
And things will never be what they seem

It started the first day my brother died
I sat on the porch step and just cried
Someone who meant so much but now is gone
It really couldn't have felt more wrong

No more competing in intense video games
Just sitting alone thinking, while it rains
No more going on adventures with the wheelchair
Walk slowly into his room and stare

Remembering all of the memories we shared

I remember when he would come to my races
Watching me set some really fast paces
I would always do better when he was there
Even though it was very rare

I remember him waking me up late at night
And me never trying to show any fright
He just wanted me to help him out
A late night talk without a shout

He was always a really strong person
Fighting his muscular dystrophy with assertion
Although he became weaker and weaker
He kept his head high and was still a dreamer

The night my life changed was unexpected
I thought my brother was getting well rested
Turns out he was in a deep sleep
One he never came out of or seeked

I laid next to him thinking what it would be like
A life without Myles, a brother no longer by my side
I knew all along he would be in a better place
And he definitely didn't leave this world without a trace

The thing that tore me apart the most
Was seeing him one last time before he goes

Sean's Poem

I never really got a final goodbye
It saddens me because his heart was so close to mine
He's been gone since 2002
It's crazy how much time has flew
Myles was an amazing friend to me
If you had a chance to know him, you would see.

Through Myles' Eyes

As *No Wheelchairs in Heaven* was going to press, I received this letter from a man who received one of Myles' corneas. The letter was pure gift—a way to finish the story of the gift of Myles' life. With permission from the South Dakota Lions Eye Bank, his letter is reprinted below.

>Let me start by telling you and your family that I received one of your son Myles' corneas. I had an eye condition called kerakatonis (the spelling is probably wrong). My vision was getting to the point that my right eye was very blurry and could not be corrected by normal methods. Since the transplant, my vision has improved greatly. I take eye drops twice daily, so I never forget that I owe Myles for my better vision!
>
>Here is a brief description about myself. I am currently 46 and have a wife and two kids. My daughter is 13, and my son is 15. They are both active in sports, so having good vision really helps me enjoy watching them play.

My interests are hunting, fishing, camping, taking care of my lawn, old cars (I have 3 projects). I enjoy watching all Minnesota pro and college sports.

I have worked at the same job for 26 years, and I am currently the buyer.

I have always wanted to contact you about the gift of my cornea, but never felt the time was right.

Please comfort yourself in knowing that Myles, in some way, is now seeing the world through me. He will enjoy all nature can deliver as I am a very active person. Since Myles was in a wheelchair, I would think I have taken him to places he could not imagine!

You can feel good that his cornea went to a good, friendly, religious, and well-liked person.

Thanks, Myles,
Dan

LaVergne, TN USA
12 April 2011
223855LV00002B/11/P